Where Do Puddles Go?

By Fay Robinson

Consultants

Robert L. Hillerich, Professor Emeritus,
Bowling Green State University, Bowling Green, Ohio;
Consultant, Pinellas County Schools, Florida

Lynne Kepler, Educational Consultant

CHILDRENS PRESS®

CHICAGO

Design by Herman Adler Design Group
Photo Research by Feldman & Associates, Inc.

Library of Congress Cataloging-in-Publication Data

Robinson, Fay.
    Where do puddles go? / by Fay Robinson.
      p. cm. – (Rookie read-about science)
    ISBN 0-516-46036-6
    1. Meteorology—Juvenile literature. 2. Water—Juvenile
literature. [1. Water. 2. Hydrologic cycle.] I. Title. II. Series.
QC863.5.R63   1995
551.57–dc20   94-35629
                                          CIP
                                          AC

24 25 26 27 28 R 11   **62**

Do you like to watch the rain pour down from the sky, soaking trees and plants and streets and sidewalks?

Then, right after it rains, do you ever put on your boots and jump in the puddles?

When the sun comes out,
everything dries up,

and the puddles disappear.
Where do they go?

Puddles dry up because of the sun. Heat from the sun warms the smallest parts of each drop of water.

Warm air rises, and the tiny bits of water rise, too. They become part of the air. This is called evaporation.

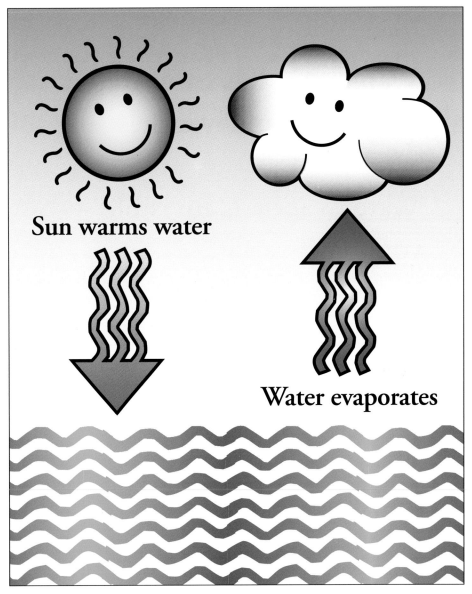

Sun warms water

Water evaporates

Water that has evaporated is called water vapor.

Water vapor is invisible — you can't see it.

If you can't see it, how do you know it's there? Here's one way to prove it. Set a glass of ice water in the sun.

Soon, water will start
to drip down the outside
of the glass. It didn't leak
out of the glass; it's water
that was in the air.

When water vapor is
cooled, it turns back
into water. This is
called condensation.

Water vapor rises high into the sky.

The air is cooler up there, so the water vapor condenses. Tiny water droplets join with other droplets, and soon there are so many droplets in one place that you can see them.

That's what clouds are.

There are different kinds
of clouds. Some are big
and puffy and white.

Some are so full of water that they turn gray. Then, heavy drops of water fall to the ground as rain.

If it is cold enough outside,
it snows instead.

Rainwater doesn't always evaporate right away. A lot of it trickles into streams and rivers.

The streams and rivers
flow into lakes and oceans.
The sun heats them up
like giant puddles.

Water on the surface
evaporates, rises into
the sky, collects as clouds,
and falls as rain again.

This pattern is called
the water cycle.

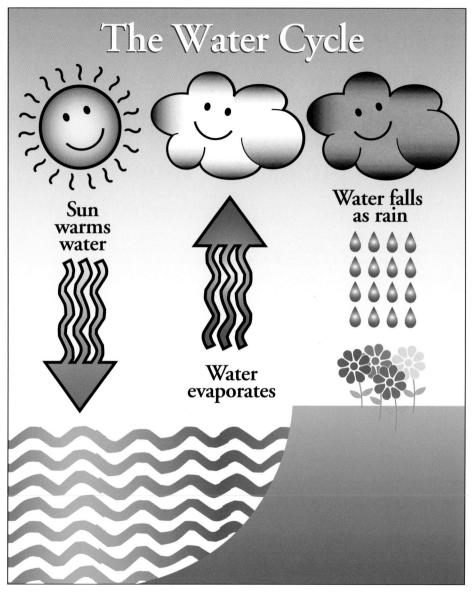

The Water Cycle

Sun
warms
water

Water
evaporates

Water falls
as rain

The water cycle never stops. All the water we have on Earth is all we ever had. From prehistoric times until now, the same water is used over and over and over again.

That's one good reason
to take care of it.

The water you use today

may someday fall in a mountain snowstorm,

crash over a cliff in a waterfall,

spout from a whale
in an ocean,

or fill a puddle you jump
in right after it rains.